THE COLLIERY

THE COLLIERY

by

Dennis Hamilton

Basiljet Books
Hampshire, UK

First published in the UK by Basiljet Books

ISBN 978-0-9558478-2-0

THE COLLIERY

❧

INTRODUCTION

Heartfelt thanks are due to the people of North Seaton Colliery, Newbiggin-by-the-Sea, and Ashington, Northumberland, without whose help this book would not have been possible.

A special thanks must go to Mr John Clark (senior) whose poems (which I am both proud and privileged to incorporate in my book) have been an inspiration. They brought back many memories for me, and I'm sure they will do the same for anyone from the area who may read this book in the future. Some of the wording may be a bit (shall we say) foreign to some people, so I will do my best to clarify things as necessary.

John Clark was born on the 1 February 1935 in Pont Street, Ashington (a town adjacent to North Seaton and Newbiggin) where, in his own words, 'you not only lived but survived.' John was educated at St Aidan's RC School, Ashington and spent the majority of his working life as coal miner at Ashington Colliery until its closure in 1988.

John reminisced about his youth as follows:

A lot of families at that time (late 1930s early '40s) consisted of 7 to 11 people and trouble was rare. Doors were rarely locked, and neighbour invariably helped neighbour in any way possible. Thieving was a rarity (nothing worth stealing really) and sorted by the people (normally the bigger lads) themselves.

I know we had a policeman in North Seaton as I grew up, but I can never remember actually seeing him myself. As John says, any wrong-doing or misbehaving was sorted out between families or friends. In those days, discipline and good manners were bywords in the community.

THE AUTHOR

I was born in 1945 and spent the first 5 years of my life in a mining village called North Seaton Colliery where the greater part of my relatives lived (except for those in Scotland). Fourth son to my father (pronounced harshly without the r) a miner named John (or 'Jacky' to his workmates) and a hard-working mother (our Mam), Jane Lillian (known as Ginny). The family unit (by 1949) consisted of six siblings, my two sisters being both the eldest and youngest of them.

1951 saw my family move to a brand new council house (complete with indoor plumbing) to a town a few miles away called Newbiggin-by-the-Sea where I was to finish my schooling at the ripe old age of fifteen as a Secondary Modern student. It was an education that I came to realise later was one designed and moulded around the job prospects of the area (mining or fishing). Chances of enhanced education were very few and far between and usually reserved for the children of people like the local doctor or businessman (or so it appeared to most).

Outside of school, my childhood free-time was spent either walking by road or by the cliff path which led back to North Seaton Colliery and my grandparents, aunts, uncles, and siblings. I'm afraid the lure of the "Wanny" (River Wansbeck) for fishing and adventures was very strong.

In 1960, on leaving school, I took and passed the entrance examination for Boys' Service in the army (hoping for the chance to become a bandsman in a highland regiment) and found myself at Harrogate in Yorkshire as an apprentice in Radio Communication. Three years of trade, further education, and fitness training was to be followed by another 22 years of military service.

This, in turn, was followed by 10 years as a police officer, and then finally a number of years as a Civil Service lecturer in communications and Information Technology. I retired in 2009, and that was when I found out what work was really all about!

I settled down to write this book in the late months of 2019. It is a book that I hope will give some insight into the life that colliery folk enjoyed – the joy and the pleasure, as well as the hardships and heartache. Close-knit and insular, maybe: North Seaton Colliery nonetheless left me with wonderful memories of childhood and times past.

THE BORDERS

The north-east coast of Northumberland (or as it is known now, 'the Borders') has, and always will hold, a special place in my heart. A place of rugged beauty, castles and people with a heart of gold which could have been – but wasn't – marred with the advent of coal mining and the associated muck and grime that came with it. Fishing (although part and parcel of the area's working life) was for many an escape from the daily routine of mining and also a great supplement to a somewhat meagre diet.

Time passes, but memories of a life in a community of hard working, family-oriented, loving people – a people that I am proud to have been part of – can never be forgotten...

NORTH SEATON COLLIERY

Although North Seaton had been in existence for some years, the first recorded mining shaft was sunk in 1859 under the auspices of the Cowpen and North Seaton Coal Company. The company employed 933 miners, and in so doing turned the little village of North Seaton into a strong mining community.

Title of the pit transferred to the Cowpen mining company in 1890 and finally to the National Coal Board in 1947. At the height of its productivity (around 1950), the mine employed just under 1000 people of which around 700 worked underground.

From 1955 onwards the mine saw a gradual decrease in numbers, with miners being transferred to other pits or laid off until final closure in 1961. Since its closure, the once vibrant colliery has mostly been demolished. People moved to other outlying districts. However, the one thing that has not changed in the area is the sense of community — something that is enjoyed especially amongst the older people.

(Photo courtesy of Brian Shotton)

This partial view of North Seaton Colliery shows the single rows on the left (houses with only one large living room downstairs plus a kitchen), doubles (houses with two living rooms downstairs) in the centre, and on the right the chapel, little school, and the beginning of Chapel Row.

THE WELFARE CLUB

The Welfare Club was the main focus for relaxation in the colliery, combining many leisure and sports facilities – bowling, tennis, snooker, dance hall, and of course the proverbial 'bar' to name but a few. The nearest pub (as I recall) would have been either a bus ride away (on the North Seaton Flier) or a fair walk (about a mile) up the church path to the White Elephant.

That path had many happy and scary memories for me. On darker late afternoons in the winter, walking to and from the nearest Cinema (the Hippodrome), which was on the opposite side of the road from the White Elephant, meant taking the dimly lit path.

To say the colliery was a close-knit community would be an awful understatement as everyone seemed to know everyone else's business. When up to no good, kids (or 'bairns' as we were called) often heard the cry 'just wait till I see your Mutha/Fatha' – a cry that was often followed by a clip 'round the ear. Children of colliery families never seemed to move far away and often (like mine) would have grandparents, uncles, aunties, and cousins in close proximity.

NORTH SEATON WELFARE

Wor club it was the Welfare
The best club in the land,
We've even had the pigeon men
Doing the one man band.

One time the brewery went on strike
We found it was no joke,
Tommy and June flying aboot
For Guinness, Stout or Coke.

I've seen us all plough doon there
The snow made your nose runny,
After searching through all wor togs
We had very little money.

But the bonnie lass behind the bar
She was our one big saviour,
We would get a pint or two
For our good behaviour.

At last the welfare no longer stands
They did us something rotten,
But memories linger in our heads
For them gone, but not forgotten.

BOWLING AT THE WELFARE

Sport facilities at the club
Were the best you've ever seen,
Football, tennis, whippets and quoits
And a "first class" bowling green.

The groundsman kept them up too scratch
Jimmy Pringle was his name,
Don't let the bairns run about
They're about to start their game.

Tichy Scott and old Ned
As partner's they took some beating,
According to the record books
They were the best pair in North Seaton.

Now I've never played at bowls before
Ned Seedhouse was my buddy,
"You'd better take notice what he says
Cos he's an old stubborn cuddy."

"You're bowling far too hard"
OLD Ned would spit and splutter,
"Have ya seen where ya woods have gone
Oops another one in the gutter."

Now sad to say, its all gone to wreck and ruin
There was no more resources,
The last we heard of the bowling green
It was over run by horses.

(cuddy — horse or pony)

The Welfare was, and remained, the central hub of many activities enjoyed by the people not only from the colliery but also from the surrounding area. The sporting, cultural, and leisure activities it hosted were second to none: leek shows, pigeon racing, whippet racing, snooker/billiards, bowling, and numerous parties and dancing.

Like most clubs, the welfare had its membership although not being a member did not preclude you from using the facilities or enjoying the entertainment.

MEMBERS' FANCY DRESS

At the club tonight there's a fancy dress
Old men showing their knobbly knees,
Frank and Joyce Price at 9.30 sharp
Will serve up Pies and Peas.

Jackie and Peter with Jean and Pat
Are selling tickets for the prizes,
"If we get knobbled doing this
Hey up it's the Assizes".

Tommy Shotton and Bill Longstaff
They both dress up as "Junkies",
Billy Bell gave his "Tarzan" yell
Little Willy Doyle "his monkey".

Belle Davison was a late entry
How she caught the judges' eye,
In a St Trinian skirt and hockey stick
They presented her, first prize.

"Caravaner's" walked from Sandy Bay
Through sand and clarts their treading,
To "wor delight" at the end of the night
Was a display of their "mock wedding".

OLD FOLKS' TREAT AT NORTH SEATON

Put on your bib and tucker
Forget Coronation Street,
We're heading for the welfare
For the old folks' Xmas treat.

We'll call down Middle-Double
For Joe and Ethel Varty,
According to the list they have
They're gannin to the party.

Looking at the menu
We get a whisky neat,
Vegetables, roasted spuds
And any amount of meat.

Now for the entertainment
A chap danced in his clogs,
Followed by Harry Seymour
With a monologue about dogs.

We all danced the Gay Gordon's
And doing all or dickers,
An old wife slipped, coup her
And flashed her Xmas knickers.

The women filled with Plum Duff
The men tanked up with beer,
Now the treat has ended
We'll come again next year.

NORTH SEATON LEEK SHOW

(Photo courtesy of Brian Shotton)

Leek show at the welfare
The highlight of the year,
Yards of broth to gan at
And wa bellies full of beer.

Now Ted or Jack or Sammy
They tek the first three prizes,
Every year, a big toss-up
Who has the biggest sizes.

Old Norky Scott, he put three in
"I've grown them in a jar,"
But all the bairns joked with him
"Ahh ye got them from the Spar".

To sing a song or tell a joke
Ya name it went straight down,
We'd kick off with Dawson James
Followed by China Brown.

They'd clap and shout for Meggie Clark
A wife you nivver hustle,
First she'd de a shimmy
Her encore, show her muscles.

Now Davey Watts, a great big lad
And he could hold his ale,
"Any broth left" he'd call at time
"I've got me plastic pale".

NORTH SEATON WHIPPETS

Another favourite pastime was the whippet racing. A wee bit of illegal gambling took place on the side (shock, horror), but there was always a couple of pints to follow. Whippets are really 'full on' during their first two or three years but settle into a loving household pet later in life.

*(My daughter's whippet, "Cali" —
KC registered as Calixta South Coast)*

NORTH SEATON WHIPPETS

I'd gan and seek old Bobby Lisle
Catching him and her embracing,
"now cut that out, put on your boots
We're gannin whippet racing".

Now Clarky, Bob and wor pal Don
And even Freddie Sparrow,
We'd wheel the boxes from the club
On Seymour's two wheeled barrow.

There's always folks we're waiting for
They nivver seem too hurry,
If it's not Mat or Alan White
It's June and Colin Murray.

At last we've started racing
The dogs are in and muzzled,
The red dog traps, the owner gasp
The four other dogs looked puzzled.

They call the red dog "Ragman"
Each performance was a treat,
Even handicapped of two behind
That dog would not be beat.

Racing done, the gears away
Seymour's nipped off in his car,
But "Hoy" he shouts across the field
"I'll catch you's in the bar".

A TYPICAL SCENE

A typical scene from many mining households involved the drying of pit clothes over the fire – to get them ready quickly for the next shift, or even just because of inclement weather.

(Photo courtesy of Jeff Slaughter)

(Note the pit boots on the chair waiting to be cleaned and covered in dubbin...)

WOR BACK STREET

Thump, thump, was all you'd hear
Between preparing grub,
Some mothers doing washing
In a great big wooden tub.

Me ma she stood – strong as an ox
With her you would not tangle,
I think it had something to do
With a "poss-stick and a mangle."

The dirty clothes, brought from the pit
They did take some scrubbing,
Fustins washed, hung out to dry
The pit boots – clagged with Dubbin.

The stottie's cooling on the sill
With "cola harn" a plenty,
Hawkers shouting up the street
"One penny – just for twenty."

The mid-wife's coming on her bike
"Take the proggy mat, next door,"
She doesn't want a showing up
They've no oilcloth, on the floor.

Sunday night, me dad's asleep
But in his mind, he's planning,
Happiest man in the street
"Foreshift" – he's not gannin.

*(fustins – pit clothing; stottie – round flat bread; cola harn
– smoked herring)*

THE WANSBECK

The colliery itself was located on the North bank of the river Wansbeck, a river which played a great part in the life of the community. It was a means of relaxation for the miners and their families, (on the sand dunes especially during the summer months), a ready way to supplement the larder through fishing (although sometimes not through conventional methods), and a wonderful playground full of exiting places and things to explore for the children.

FLATTY STABBING

If you couldn't afford hooks
Or cord wrapped on a stick,
A four pronged fork on a stick
Would help to do the trick.

You plodge down by the red bridge
Not far from Sandy Bay,
The big ones is what you want
The small ones let away.

If you caught a good few
You'd share some with your mate,
Or give some to the fishermen
They'd use them for pot-bait.

You always kept the spotted ones
Cause they are nice and sweet,
But if they swim near to you
Mind you don't prog your feet.

You had to be quite wary
Of crabs and conga eels,
The doggers nipped at your big toes
The congas bite your heels.

With a bottle of water
And "doorsteps" off your mam,
You couldn't wait too scoff them down
No margarine, just jam.

(plodge — paddle; dogger — large crab)

One of the other 'fishing implements' we used was the trusted garden cane with a six inch nail at the end tied with cord. This was placed between the big and next toe and pushed down when the flatfish were felt underfoot. Wading or 'plodging' on the sandbanks could be quite dangerous if you didn't keep an eye on the rising tide. This was because the gulleys at the sides of the sandbanks were usually two or three feet deeper (and the current stronger) than the sand you were fishing on.

(The Trot — Photo courtesy of John Dawson)

The red bridge mentioned in the previous poem (more commonly known as 'The Trot' was a construction that was used to ferry tubs of coal from the colliery to Cambois power station on the other side of the Wansbeck. It also provided a means of crossing the river for the lawless few who wanted to get to Wheatley's Ferry (renowned by some as one of the best fishing spots). Maintenance was not one of its best features, and the dangers of crossing it (mindful of any mine workers) was quite, shall we say, dodgy to say the least. Not only were the frayed steel hawsers and deck pulleys dangerous, but also the wooden decking which could certainly have done with some repair work.

(Wheatley's Ferry — Photo courtesy of Brian Shotton)

Although the Ferry fell into disuse some years ago, the height above water at high tide made it an ideal perch for the avid fisherman (or boy, in my case). It was quite the adventure for the young to get over the Trot and through the bushes to the ferry.

Of course, it wasn't only the kids who used to risk their necks crossing the Trot.

FISHING – DOON NORTH SEATON

It's "Yem" from school
Dinners on me plate,
Gobbled it "Doon"
"Divvent" want to be late.

With me mate, and me Dad
We're away fishing,
"Ti" catch quite a few
The three of us wishing.

It's hook-line-and sinker
We'll "hev – ti – tek,"
Keep on the hard sand
"Divvent" stand in the sleck

Me Dad likes his pipe
We've "Ne" time to wait,
The time he's a puffing
We'll "Gan" and dig the bait.

Now opposite the boat-house
It's the best place to be,
Ye catch the "Big Whoppers"
That come from the sea.

The sun is a setting
The tides on the flow,
"Wiv" packed up "Wa" gear
It's time for to go.

At the top of the lane
Me Mam waits with – her – dish,
But all there's to show
Is a wet arse and "nee fish."

THE CHINE – DOON NORTH SEATON

To get doon to the chine
You couldn't catch a bus,
The long walk doon there
Nivver bothered us.

If you lived in Ashington
To get doon to the sea,
You'd walk doon the church path
Or cut through Pity-Me.

The bairns would play "roonders"
Or kick a ball aboot,
"Howay your dinner's ready"
Ye could hear their mother's shoot.

A seacoal bloke passing bye
Dressed in work attire,
"Can ye spare a shull-o-coal
To put onto wa fire.

Ye could always tell the rich folk
They'd have a barbeque,
Pork pies, Jellied eels
Then finish off with stew.

Now the sun is setting
No longer can we bide,
Across the sands, up the bank
"Mek sharp, here's the tide".

(The Chine — so called because of the local dialect pronunciation of the word 'chain.' In times past an old chain link ferry used to cross the river.)

It wasn't all flatty stabbing, although they were nice fried. If perchance you managed to have a bob or two you could buy yourself a handline, sinkers (probably home made with nuts and bolts) and barbed hooks. Thankfully my father was a dab hand with pliers because being a little smarty pants and trying to throw my handline as far as possible into the river by swinging it around my head, I managed to hook not a fish but my own finger. Painful but a salutary lesson, nevertheless.

Needing to find something to bait your fishing line with was part of the fun, and searching for things like limpets, crabs (soft skins were the best) and sand worms (lugworms used to give quite a nip if you weren't careful) was just as enjoyable as the fishing itself...

(Digging for sandworms — Photo courtesy of Brian Shotton)

Some had their own boats down in the harbour, and I imagine the sea and fresh air after shifts at the mine were a great tonic. Playing around at the harbour as a child, you used to get absolutely filthy with clarts (sticky black mud) and usually ended up in bed with a sore backside and no supper.

(The Harbour at Low Tide — Photo courtesy of Brian Shotton)

THE BARREL OF BEER

Scotty and his marra'
Out for a walk one day,
Found a wooden barrel
It had fallen from the dray.

They booled it down the harbour
He shouted out with glee,
"Gan-on fetch all the lads
They can have a drink on me".

Little Nut walked to the club
He saw the cleaning lasses,
"Is June Porterhouse not here yet
I'm after some pint glasses".

There was a bit of fisticuffs
A thing we could not bide,
Tucker Young grabbed their necks
And chucked them in the tide.

There was a short discussion
On them we weren't too hard,
"But any more carry on
And you know you'll both be barred".

The Chapel folk from all around
Played war about the din,
He've they opened another bar
"Whey I, it's the Harbour Inn.

Many were the happy memories for children of the colliery, a fantastic playground around the welfare and the shore where your imagination could run riot. However, nothing surpassed the one thing that brought all the colliery families together - the Colliery Gala Day.

(Gala Day 1954 – Photo courtesy of Jeff Slaughter, Snr)

NORTH SEATON GALA DAY

The bairn's meet at the school yard
On their Gala Day,
It costs their Dad a 'tanner'
They keep it off their pay.

The colliery band would lead them
Playing all the bonny notes,
Followed by the Committee
Then the decked out floats.

Geordie Bully says to me
"Hev ye seen wor lass Minnie,
There's ne mistaken hor attal
She's bought a brand new pinnie."

When the races started
It was first past the line,
An old granddad was heard to say
"I'll bet that's one of mine."

There was roundabouts and donkey rides
The bairns they had great fun,
A bag of fruit, A Gala mug
And a great big currant bun.

It's getting dark, it's time for home
This is sad to say,
But everyone's enjoyed themselves
On North Seaton's Gala Day.

(tanner — old sixpence; pinnie — apron)

The Gala Mug, still a treasured memory for many of the colliery families, is a keepsake that you can still find lurking in some cupboards.

(Photo courtesy of my niece, Susan Wallace (nee Bullough), who was born and brought up in North Seaton Colliery)

Life certainly wasn't all cigarettes, beer, and playtime. But neither were such things begrudged to the hard-working folk. Many jobs and tasks had to be carried out to ensure the ongoing livelihood of the colliery. And one job that stuck in the minds of most colliery folk was that of cleaning out the middens.

THE MIDDENS

At two o'clock in the morning
The scrape of a size nine boot,
It was only Jack with his horse and cart
Come to clean the middens out.

They call them the box toilet
Or other pit-matic name,
Everybody had one
It wasn't such a shame.

It wasn't a flush toilet
These were built before the war,
You sat spying through the knot hole
Or just hiding from your Ma.

It was a smelly task no doubt
To Jack it was just a job,
Someone had to do it
To earn a few meagre bob.

The middens cleaned and dusted
Jack feeling proud and grand,
"Bess don't go messing up the street
Horse-muck I cannot stand".

The horse now fed and watered
Home for a nice hot bath,
He'll be back again on Monday
To clean up the aftermath.

Things did get better with the advent of flushing toilets which were still outside (and boy were they cold) alongside the coal bunker from which you could earn a bob or two shovelling in the coal when the loads arrived.

(Photo courtesy of Brian Shotton)

Another way of earning a few extra bob to supplement the household (plus extra beer and cigarette money) was to take on a little extra back-breaking work such as helping the local farmer with his potato harvest. Poaching was also profitable, especially if you didn't get caught...

TETTIE PICKING

I thought I'd earn some extra cash
So I put on my old duds,
Following the tractor
To harvest "Peace's" spuds.

Wilf was a hard taskmaster
Your back would ache with pain,
Get those tetties all picked up
Never mind the rain.

I thought I'd take a boiling
Hope Wilfy wouldn't mind,
But galloping across the field
Came "Jack Young – Peace's" hind.

Coming down the Boiler road
The copper on his bike,
How unlucky can you get
For me I had to hike.

"Now the tetties that you got
I hope you didn't steal,
Or did you just borrow them
To go towards a meal".

"This time it's just a warning"
In me he put big fear,
He undid his big blue cape
And bashed me round the ear.

ABOUT OLD TUCKER

Old Tucker Young — a red faced bloke
He lives down Wansbeck Street,
A jolly kind of fellow
You'd ever wished to meet.

Often down the river
For salmon — he would net,
The bailiffs have tried for years
They haven't caught him yet.

He likes to go out catching birds
With cages and his nets,
He never sells a wild bird
Keeps them all for pets.

He tamed an old wife's dog one week
It turned out quite a savage,
He put it on a diet
Of water and raw cabbage.

Tuck didn't like the pit at all
To go, was rather hard,
"That's me void the morn" he'd say
"I've won a domino card".

A lot of water under the bridge
Eighty years, he is approaching,
But give him half a chance
He'd be away out poaching.

John didn't just write poems about the life of folks in the North Seaton area, but also his personal thoughts. It is these thoughts that I would now like to share. It is with regret and sorrow that whilst in the middle of compiling this book John Clark passed away. This then becomes a eulogy to John as well as (what I consider) a memory of the colliery and its people. However, I take heart from knowing that his poetry will forever be a lasting memory of the man and his life.

GRANDA'S HELPER

"Where's my Grandad?" you would ask
When coming for a visit
A rat — a — tat on the garden shed
Then I'd shout "Who is it?"

You'd put on your small apron
And help me make some toys,
A dollies house for a little
And soldier's forts for boys.

I'd love the way you'd screw your face
As I'd watch you through the door,
Trying to cut a piece of wood
With your little plastic saw.

Have you swept the sawdust
Cleaned and oiled your tool,
Don't forget on Monday
That you'll be starting school.

I saw you sitting with your friend
The school bus would soon depart,
A little tear ran down your cheek
It nearly broke my heart.

Your mammy says that you liked school
Some lessons are a bore,
You cannot wait for the weekend
To rattle the shed door.

FRIENDSHIP

Walk along a country lane
As the day is dawning,
Pass a stranger on the path
Simply say "Good Morning".

The paper boy on his daily round
A sighing and a yawning,
Help to brighten up his day
Simply say "Good Morning".

The sun climbs slowly overhead
The time it passes soon,
A lady hanging out her clothes
Just say "Good Afternoon".

Two little words of friendship
Will help to break the ice,
Takes nothing to be sociable
Courteous or nice.

Climb the stairs, off too bed
Time to dim the light,
Kiss your loved one on the cheek
And simply say "Good Night"

LONELINESS

Sat here in my cottage
Another lonely day,
Children grown up and married
They've all moved away.

A week of their school holidays
The grand-children come to stay,
I break my heart in silence
When they have to go away.

No-one to say hello to
No smiling face to see,
No letters lying on the mat
Saying "hello mam it's me".

Looking out my window
A great big world I see,
Are there people, out there
Lonely just like me.

Staring at the four grey walls
My heart is filled with sorrow,
A cup of tea, away to be
Perhaps they'll call tomorrow.

DREAMING

Queerest things go through my head
While resting in my comfy bed,
Am I dead or just asleep
Please come in and take a peep.

An angel called me through the night
Hand in hand we both took flight,
Past the moon, A shooting star
His smiling face, it isn't far.

Leading me on to meet my maker
Lord above the world creator,
Sitting there for you He waits
Just inside the pearly gates.

I see the family all around
The crying and the wailing sound,
Why oh why, did it have to be
God has taken you from me.

A cold sweat running down my face
I wake up in my resting place,
On my cheeks, smiles a beaming
Thank you Lord, I'm only dreaming.

SLOWLY DYING

The North Sea and Atlantic
Flowing from both sides,
Eat away the surrounding cliffs
With their raging tides.

Oh our beloved England
Mother of the free
Disappearing far to fast
Swallowed by the sea.

No more picnics on the sands
Or children's donkey rides,
Beaches gone forever
Covered by the tides.

Save us God Almighty
We place our trust in thee,
Stop all the erosion
And perils from the sea.

Years from now I wonder
Where will England be,
With its green and pleasant land
Will it all be in the sea.

THE NEWCASTLE TRIP

A bus trip leaving Saturday night
So put your name straight down,
To the Spring Bank Social Club
It's just outside the town.

They make you feel right welcome
We've been there twice before,
The Committee and old friends
Would greet you at the door.

"Your entertainment here tonight
Please sit yourselves at ease,
I'd like to call on Peter Payne
To start the "Go-as-you-please".

With five professionals on the show
Was something he had to beat,
But with his favourite Jim Reeve's song
It went down quite a treat.

When a judge announced the winner
We could tell, looking at his face,
Jim Reeve's song had done him proud
It got him second place.

On the Homeward journey
A little voice in the middle,
"Can you stop the bus for five
I have to have a tiddle".

Little Jean's hubby, like a flash
"Can I help you over the gate"
"Get yourself back on the bus
You've passed your sell by date".

(John Clark)

Although I never had the pleasure of meeting John face-to-face, we did correspond and have telephone conversations. He was, as ever, most courteous and helpful to me. I'm sure, like me, his family and friends will miss him greatly and I hope I have done him some small favour in printing his poems.

Thank you.